Beginning the Walk

JESUS
THE LIFE

Ron and Mary Bennett

A NavPress resource published in alliance with Tyndale House Publishers, Inc.

NavPress is the publishing ministry of The Navigators, an international Christian organization and leader in personal spiritual development. NavPress is committed to helping people grow spiritually and enjoy lives of meaning and hope through personal and group resources that are biblically rooted, culturally relevant, and highly practical.

For more information, visit www.NavPress.com.

Beginning the Walk: Jesus–The Life

Copyright © 2004 by The Navigators, Navigator Church Ministries. All rights reserved.

A NavPress resource published in alliance with Tyndale House Publishers, Inc.

NCM and the NCM logo are trademarks of The Navigators, Colorado Springs, CO. *NAVPRESS* and the NAVPRESS logo are registered trademarks of NavPress, The Navigators, Colorado Springs, CO. *TYNDALE* is a registered trademark of Tyndale House Publishers, Inc. Absence of ® in connection with marks of NavPress or other parties does not indicate an absence of registration of those marks.

Cover design by Arvid Wallen
Cover imagery by Arvid Wallen
Creative Team: Bob Walz, Steve Parolini, Arvid Wallen, Kathy Mosier, Glynese Northam, Pat Reinheimer

Navigator Church Ministries (NCM) is focused on helping churches become more intentional in disciplemaking. NCM staff nationwide are available to help churches grow an intentional disciplemaking culture that will enable them to accomplish Christ's Great Commission. For further information on how NCM can help you, please call (719) 594-2446.

Some of the anecdotal illustrations in this book are true to life and are included with the permission of the persons involved. All other illustrations are composites of real situations, and any resemblance to people living or dead is coincidental.

Scripture quotations marked *THE MESSAGE* are taken from *THE MESSAGE* by Eugene H. Peterson, copyright © 1993, 1994, 1995, 1996, 2000, 2001, 2002. Used by permission of NavPress Publishing Group. All rights reserved. Scripture quotations marked NASB are taken from the New American Standard Bible,® copyright © 1960, 1962, 1963, 1968, 1971, 1972, 1973, 1975, 1977, 1995 by The Lockman Foundation. Used by permission. Scripture quotations marked NIV are taken from the Holy Bible, *New International Version,*® *NIV.*® Copyright © 1973, 1978, 1984, 2011 by Biblica, Inc.® Used by permission. All rights reserved worldwide. Scripture quotations marked TLB are taken from *The Living Bible,* copyright © 1971 by Tyndale House Foundation. Used by permission of Tyndale House Publishers, Inc., Carol Stream, Illinois 60188. All rights reserved.

ISBN 978-1-57683-708-5

For further information regarding this material and other discipling resources contact:

The Navigators
P.O. Box 6000
Colorado Springs, CO 80934
www.navigators.org/ncm

About Beginning the Walk

This study is part of a three-book series called *Beginning the Walk*. These studies are designed to help believers begin their new life with Christ. Although intended for individual use, they can also be used with a mentor or in a small group. However you use this series, you won't need an extensive church or religious background to get started. Each study begins right where you are — with the basics. The series includes the following three studies:

- *Jesus: The Way*
- *Jesus: The Truth*
- *Jesus: The Life*

We recommend you begin with the book *Jesus: The Way*. Each study contains six lessons with a key Scripture verse at the beginning of each lesson. A lesson will probably take thirty to forty-five minutes to complete, but don't feel bound by that time frame. If you get through them faster, that's okay. And if you spend more time in each lesson, that's okay too.

The Bible passages used in this series are included in the text of the lessons. Still, we highly recommend you have a personal Bible as well. In addition to reading the Scripture in the lesson, you may want to look up the references and read them in your own Bible. This will broaden your understanding as you discover more about the context of the Scripture passages.

Contents

ACKNOWLEDGMENT 7

INTRODUCTION 9

LESSON 1: FAITH 11
Faith allows us to see the invisible reality of God's kingdom, it is the means by which we relate to God, and it inspires us to face the unknown with certainty.

LESSON 2: THE WORD 19
The Bible is God's way of revealing Himself to us and serves as a how-to-live manual.

LESSON 3: PRAYER 28
Prayer is our personal communication with the living God.

LESSON 4: THE HOLY SPIRIT 36
Working with our spirits, the Holy Spirit teaches and comforts us as we journey through life with Christ.

LESSON 5: GRACE 45
Grace is the foundation for our security with God, the source of forgiveness, and the power to live as we should.

LESSON 6: COMMUNITY 54
God has designed His followers to live and travel with companions in community.

SUMMARY 61

ABOUT THE AUTHORS 62

Acknowledgment

We want to express our appreciation to Bob Walz for his outstanding coaching and invaluable advice in the development of this material. His insight and encouragement were a constant source of energy and motivation.

Introduction

One of the great memories I have from my childhood is a canoe trip I took with my dad and cousin into the Boundary Waters of Canada. We had done some basic family camping before, but this was the "big one." This was like going out with Lewis and Clark.

Wisely, my dad decided to break with the tradition of outfitting ourselves with only what we had or could borrow. Instead, he hired an outfitter to put together the equipment and supplies for our backwoods adventure. It was expensive and seemed extravagant in light of my dad's frugal mindset, but he reasoned, "It's a once-in-a-lifetime trip, so maybe it's better to be safe than sorry."

We arrived at the outfitter's northern outpost mid-afternoon. It was warm and sunny, and my excitement was indescribable. The canoes were already loaded on the truck. We threw in the four large duffle bags of supplies that were provided for us and drove off with the outfitter to our launch point.

This was to be a seven-day round-trip through the chain of lakes that make up the Minnesota and Canadian Boundary Waters, and we would be guided by only a map, a compass, and our courage. The outfitter left us with the parting words, "I'll be back in seven days to pick you up. Everything you need is in those duffle bags." Our last contact with civilization drove away down the dusty gravel road. We pushed off into the unknown. As far as we knew, we would not see another human being for seven days.

The content of those duffle bags was the last thing on my mind as we glided across the clear, azure blue water in search of our first portage. Those bags at that moment were simply cushions against the aluminum frame of the canoe. Who had time to consider them? We were three guys living on the wild side!

It was during our first portage that I became curious about their contents. Two hundred yards of dragging the bags uphill over rocks as we hiked made me wonder what made them so heavy. Did we really need it all? Had they given us supplies for a month instead of seven days? What if we hid one of the bags in a tree and picked it up on our return trip? But, no. Dad, convinced that everything we had was essential, made sure each item was carefully repacked as we completed each subsequent portage.

I can't remember which came first, the darkness or the rain, but both were intimidating. Looking for a suitable campsite at night in a thunderstorm made even my dad a little nervous. We eventually came upon a small island that, compared to struggling against the wind and whitecaps, seemed like a reasonable choice. Soaked, cold, and hungry, we unpacked the canoes and dragged the equipment to a clearing on a rocky ledge.

"I wonder if they packed a tent?" I remember asking. "I'm sure they did," my dad replied. "I just hope we can figure out how to put it up!" I hadn't even thought of that. If there *were* instructions, the middle of the night in the middle of a lake in the middle of a storm was not a good time to start reading them!

Eventually we found, unpacked, and set up the tent. Three wet, hungry, and tired bodies crawled into the relative safety of our shelter held down from the gusting wind by a hasty pile of stones in lieu of tent stakes, which we discovered didn't work well on solid rock.

With our supplies safely stored and under the illumination of a small flashlight, we began to explore the contents of our four duffle bags. We looked like three raccoons foraging for food in a picnic basket. We discovered food, matches, fuel, a knife, a hatchet, and rain ponchos. It was a little late for the ponchos, but we agreed we'd use them in the next storm. Other items were carefully noted, dried, and repacked for later use.

Seven days later we met our outfitter at the prearranged pick-up point and headed back to civilization. Everything we needed during our journey had been in those duffle bags. Evidently the one who packed our supplies had made the trip before. As it turned out, there was no extra weight in the bags.

In a similar way, Christ has made the journey before us and has packed our faith-journey's duffle bags. Everything we need for our adventure with Him is included. In the following lessons, we'll take a brief look into those duffle bags at some of the essential supplies we'll need for this incredible journey called life.

Knowing what's available can make setting up camp less threatening. But if you don't understand it all right now, that's okay. Your guide has not only packed your bags, but He is also traveling with you. Christ is your outfitter *and* guide. He has been down the road before, and nothing you encounter will be a surprise to Him.

In this book we will look at our resources of:

- Faith
- The Word
- Prayer
- The Holy Spirit
- Grace
- Community

LESSON 1

Faith

NEXT STEPS

Faith is essential to our journey with Christ. It is the currency of God's kingdom. It takes us every place we need to go. Faith allows us to see the invisible reality of God's kingdom, it is the means by which we relate to God, and it inspires us to face the unknown with certainty.

> *Trust in the LORD with all your heart*
> *and lean not on your own understanding;*
> *in all your ways acknowledge him,*
> *and he will make your paths straight.*
>
> PROVERBS 3:5-6, NIV

In the 1960s, space interest reached an all-time high as the Russians launched the orbiting unmanned satellite Sputnik. America was playing catch-up but eventually made plans to place men on the moon. It was in that environment that I began my undergraduate study in aerospace engineering.

In one of our courses, we were given an assignment to design a vehicle that astronauts could use to explore the surface of the moon. Because we had no firsthand knowledge of the composition of the moon's surface (we did know it wasn't made of cheese), the vehicle needed to be able to handle any kind of surface and terrain. What we came up with was akin to an early prototype of an all-terrain vehicle (ATV).

ATVs today are only remotely similar to our class project or even to the actual moon explorer. But they serve the same purpose. Mary and I rode an ATV over a twelve-thousand-foot mountain pass in Colorado. On our journey we encountered every kind of terrain possible — water, rocks, dirt, sand, and snow. Part of the adventure was learning to trust the capability of our vehicle. As we conquered each obstacle, we grew more confident for the next.

Our life with Christ requires faith from beginning to end. It is our vehicle for traveling on this incredible journey. It is essential and is not something we outgrow. The more we understand about faith, the more we will come to rely on its power for daily living.

Faith and Reality

The word *faith*, like so many words in our culture, can have many meanings. It's often used to convey optimism. We say to someone who is facing the unknown, "Just have faith." Sometimes it refers to a whole body of religious teaching, such as, "They were strong in their faith."

When the Bible uses the term *faith*, it is referring to a trust in something *real, yet unseen* that inspires action in the direction of that belief. The book of Hebrews explains it well: "The fundamental fact of existence is that this trust in God, this faith, is the firm foundation under everything that makes life worth living. It's our handle on what we can't see" (11:1).

Q1. What does this passage say about faith?

Biblical faith is more than optimism. Biblical faith is not a dream or pretending. Dreams deal with what we hope will happen. Faith deals with what is happening but is simply not visible or seen . . . yet. It is more than a set of religious beliefs; it is a confident trust built on God, His character, and His Word.

Faith and God

If I said, "Trust me," what I'd really be saying is, "You can count on me to keep my promise." However, though I may have good intentions, I might lack the ability or opportunity to do what I promised. Therefore your faith in me, although sincere, would lack a reliable source. Faith must have a reliable object or source for trust.

The Peanuts comic strip featured a recurring scenario in which Lucy would hold a football for Charlie Brown to kick. In each cartoon Lucy talked Charlie into trusting her to hold the ball. In each cartoon she pulled it away at the last minute. And in each cartoon Charlie Brown ended up on his backside, vowing never to trust her again. But the optimistic Charlie put his faith in Lucy time after time.

Fortunately, biblical faith doesn't rely on a "Lucy" as its foundation. Biblical faith is always based on God and His Word. Look at this statement from Hebrews 11:6: "And without faith it is impossible to please God, because anyone who comes to him must believe that he exists and that he rewards those who earnestly seek him" (NIV).

Q2. What does this passage tell us is essential in order for us to please God?

Q3. Why is trust in God necessary to please Him?

If our faith is not based on God's Word or His character, it may be optimism or positive thinking — but it is not biblical faith. When God speaks, we can count on it. God has not only the desire but also the ability to keep His word. When God makes a promise, He wants us to believe it and act in light of it.

Ultimately our faith in God comes down to our trust in His character. The more we understand and experience God in our lives, the greater our confidence becomes. As we see God keep His promises, our trust in His character grows. Our spiritual lives mature as we "taste and see that the LORD is good" and realize that "blessed is the man who takes refuge in him" (Psalm 34:8, NIV).

When Charlton Heston was filming the classic movie *Ben Hur*, he did most of his own stunts, including the famous and dangerous chariot race. Legend has it that at the conclusion of his training and practice, Heston expressed to the trainer his concern that in the actual filming he might not be good enough to win the race. The trainer replied that if Heston would make sure he stayed in the chariot, the trainer would make sure he won. Faith is putting trust or confidence in someone other than ourselves who has the ability to do all that he says he'll do.

Faith and Action

Real faith always involves a response; it prompts us to move in the direction of our trust. When we have faith in God, we trust Him to do what He says He'll do, and we take steps of action in accordance with that belief. We may not always feel safe as we take these steps of faith, but our feelings are often a poor indicator of truth. It's true that faith does involve risk, particularly because we are reaching beyond our own resources and ability for what God has promised. But this is not a static amount of risk. In fact, our willingness to risk increases as our understanding of God grows.

Jesus often taught about faith during His ministry. His initial followers frequently struggled to understand this concept. During one of Jesus' teaching sessions, two very different people came to Him, and their actions helped to clarify what faith is. Read the story of Jairus and the woman in this passage from Luke and look for answers to the questions that follow.

> On his return, Jesus was welcomed by a crowd. They were all there expecting him. A man came up, Jairus by name. He was president of the meeting place. He fell at Jesus' feet and begged him to come to his home because his twelve-year-old daughter, his only child, was dying. Jesus went with him, making his way through the pushing, jostling crowd.
>
> In the crowd that day there was a woman who for twelve years had been afflicted with hemorrhages. She had spent every penny she had on doctors but not one had been able to help her. She slipped in from behind and touched the edge of Jesus' robe. At that very moment her hemorrhaging stopped. Jesus said, "Who touched me?"
>
> When no one stepped forward, Peter said, "But Master, we've got crowds of people on our hands. Dozens have touched you."
>
> Jesus insisted, "Someone touched me. I felt power discharging from me."
>
> When the woman realized that she couldn't remain hidden, she knelt trembling before him. In front of all the people, she blurted out her story — why she touched him and how at that same moment she was healed.
>
> Jesus said, "Daughter, you took a risk trusting me, and now you're healed and whole. Live well, live blessed!"

While he was still talking, someone from the leader's [Jairus's] house came up and told him, "Your daughter died. No need now to bother the Teacher."

Jesus overheard and said, "Don't be upset. Just trust me and everything will be all right." Going into the house, he wouldn't let anyone enter with him except Peter, John, James, and the child's parents.

Everyone was crying and carrying on over her. Jesus said, "Don't cry. She didn't die; she's sleeping." They laughed at him. They knew she was dead.

Then Jesus, gripping her hand, called, "My dear child, get up." She was up in an instant, up and breathing again! He told them to give her something to eat. Her parents were ecstatic, but Jesus warned them to keep quiet. "Don't tell a soul what happened in this room." (8:40-56)

Q4. How did Jairus and the woman each demonstrate faith?

Q5. What beliefs prompted their actions?

Q6. What risks did each person take?

Q7. Why do you think Jesus exposed the woman's faith publicly?

Q8. How did Jesus describe unseen reality?

One of the unique aspects of our walk with Christ is that faith makes us all equal. Background, status, position, and natural abilities are irrelevant to God. The two people in the story you just read had vastly different lifestyles. Yet they both related to Jesus personally through faith. Our common ground in Christ is faith.

Faith also allows us to live in unseen reality. Electricity is an unseen reality that we now take for granted — it's a power that remains invisible until we take the action of plugging into it. Jairus and the woman in the story had to "plug in" to Christ and His power as well.

Hebrews 11:6 makes it clear that having faith is essential to pleasing God. God always responds to faith in Him. Though we begin our walk with Christ by faith, too often we try to continue that relationship on the basis of merit. We think erroneously that while faith was adequate to get us started, it's not enough to keep God's favor. Don't make this mistake. From beginning to end, the journey with Christ is by faith.

Faith brings miraculous peace to the stormy seasons of life. Your walk with Christ won't eliminate the tensions and pain of life in a broken world, but you can be at peace even if your world is in chaos. Sometimes God stills the storms, and other times He carries us through them.

Hebrews 11:13-40 describes some of the biblical heroes of faith who, despite difficult circumstances in life, maintained their faith in God and found peace.

Each one of these people of faith died not yet having in hand what was promised, but still believing. How did they do it? They saw it way off in the distance, waved their greeting, and accepted the fact that they were transients in this world. People who live this way make it plain that they are looking for their true home. If they were homesick for the old country, they could have gone back any time they wanted. But they were after a far better country than that — *heaven* country. You can see why God is so proud of them, and has a City waiting for them.

By faith, Abraham, at the time of testing, offered Isaac back to God. Acting in faith, he was as ready to return the promised son, his only son, as he had been to receive him — and this after he had already been told, "Your descendants shall come from Isaac." Abraham figured that if God wanted to, he could raise the dead. In a sense, that's what happened when he received Isaac back, alive from off the altar.

By an act of faith, Isaac reached into the future as he blessed Jacob and Esau.

By an act of faith, Jacob on his deathbed blessed each of Joseph's sons in turn, blessing them with God's blessing, not his own — as he bowed worshipfully upon his staff.

By an act of faith, Joseph, while dying, prophesied the exodus of Israel, and made arrangements for his own burial.

By an act of faith, Moses' parents hid him away for three months after his birth. They saw the child's beauty, and they braved the king's decree.

By faith, Moses, when grown, refused the privileges of the Egyptian royal house. He chose a hard life with God's people rather than an opportunistic soft life of sin with the oppressors. He valued suffering in the Messiah's camp far greater than Egyptian wealth because he was looking ahead, anticipating the payoff. By an act of faith, he turned his heel on Egypt, indifferent to the king's blind rage. He had his eye on the One no eye can see, and kept right on going. By an act of faith, he kept the Passover Feast and sprinkled Passover blood on each house so that the destroyer of the firstborn wouldn't touch them.

> By an act of faith, Israel walked through the Red Sea on dry ground. The Egyptians tried it and drowned.
>
> By faith, the Israelites marched around the walls of Jericho for seven days, and the walls fell flat.
>
> By an act of faith, Rahab, the Jericho harlot, welcomed the spies and escaped the destruction that came on those who refused to trust God.

Q9. How did each of these people demonstrate faith?

Q10. Which one do you admire the most? Why?

SUMMARY

Faith is not wishful thinking or spiritual optimism. It is belief in the unseen reality that God has promised. Faith is only as sure as the object of the faith. As Christians, our faith is in the unchanging character and Word of God. This kind of faith results in responsive action.

PRAYER

Father, I believe that You are absolutely reliable. I can count on every word You have spoken, every promise You have made. When the future looks uncertain, when my heart begins to fear, or when confusion tries to overwhelm me, I will hold on to You as my rock, my fortress, and my secure foundation.

LESSON 2

The Word

NEXT STEPS

The Bible is God's personal Word to us. It is absolutely true and reliable. It is God's way of revealing Himself to us and serves as a how-to-live manual. As we understand it, believe it, and apply it to our lives, we will experience its power and benefits.

> *I am but a pilgrim here on earth: how I need a map — and your commands are my chart and guide. I long for your instructions more than I can tell.*
> PSALM 119:19-20, TLB

On September 11, 1777, George Washington prepared to defend Philadelphia from the British army led by General Howe. Both Washington and Howe were fighting in unfamiliar territory along Brandywine Creek. Washington's plan was not only to defend Philadelphia but also to take the offensive and surround Howe's army. His strategy was based on the location of river crossings along Brandywine Creek as noted on the maps he had been given.

Washington almost met disaster during the night as Howe's army crossed above Washington's right flank at a point called Jeffries Ford. Washington's map showed Jeffries Ford ten miles north of his army's position. In reality it was only two miles north. Washington had a solid strategy, but it was based on inaccurate maps. Only a hasty retreat saved the fragile American army from certain defeat.

Nothing is more critical when traveling in unfamiliar territory than an accurate map. An accurate map not only tells us the best route to our destination, but it also tells us what we can expect to encounter along the way. The Bible is God's road map for our walk with Christ.

The Bible is an amazing book. It is not a novel, although it contains some dramatic stories. It is not an encyclopedia, although it deals with every critical area of life. The Bible, also called Scripture or the Word, is made up of sixty-six books and divided into two major sections referred to as the Old and New Testaments. Forty different writers wrote the Bible over a 1,500-year period. The authors were kings, prophets, peasants, fishermen, poets, and philosophers. Yet with all this diversity, the Bible carries a common theme and unity throughout. This amazing unity suggests that there was one true Author... God Himself.

With regard to history, the Bible continues to be remarkable. The city of Jericho (mentioned in the Old Testament) was part of Israel's story. Undiscovered until 1930, the ruins of Jericho were finally found buried beneath the desert sand at the very location given in the Bible. The walls of the city had fallen outward as the Bible described, rather than inward as would be suggested by an invasion.

There are over three hundred prophecies (or God-given predictions) referring to Christ, the coming Messiah, in the Old Testament. Written hundreds of years before Christ, all three hundred came true. The mathematical probability that these prophecies would all be fulfilled in one man is staggering and would be impossible apart from the divine authorship of a Sovereign God.

God's preservation of the Bible over the past 3,500 years is further remarkable evidence of its divine authorship. Up until 1947, the earliest manuscripts we had of the Bible were from the ninth and tenth century. Although these handwritten documents encompassed only the first five books of the Bible, they gave incredible verification of the Bible's accuracy as a work of ancient writing.

But in 1947 in a cave near the Dead Sea, manuscripts of every Old Testament book except Esther were found and determined to be from 125 BC. Amazingly preserved, these documents were compared with those written 1,000 years later. Very few differences were discovered, and those that were had no impact on the text's meaning. This suggests that God not only gave the words originally but also preserved His words throughout history so that we might have an accurate and authoritative record of His message today.

Q1. Which of the following best describes what you believe the Bible to be?
    _____ A book of myths and fables
    _____ A book of ancient sacred writings that are no longer relevant
    _____ A book with some good, practical advice

_____ A unique book that is from God and is reliably true
_____ Other _____

_____
_____

Q2. Why (or how) did you develop that view?

The Bible and Truth

The Bible is true not because it rates high in opinion polls or fits current philosophy, but because God said it is true. Read what it says in 2 Peter 1:20-21: "For no prophecy recorded in Scripture was ever thought up by the prophet himself. It was the Holy Spirit within these godly men who gave them true messages from God" (TLB).

The Bible claims that when it speaks on a subject, it speaks truth. Jesus verified that the Old Testament was authentic and true. He quoted Old Testament Scripture frequently and based His ministry on it. He said everything that was promised in the Scriptures would come true. Jesus said, "Sanctify them by the truth; your [God's] word is truth" (John 17:17, NIV).

The Bible has been the focus of great criticism, skepticism, and persecution throughout history. Yet it continues to prove itself true in every generation. It is an anchor in a stormy sea of confusion. The truth of the Bible stands in contrast to the culture of relativism. When other philosophies have come and gone, the Bible will remain. Jesus said, "Heaven and earth will pass away, but my words will never pass away" (Mark 13:31, NIV).

The Bible is the progressive revelation of who God is and how He relates to people. The Bible doesn't tell us everything there is to know about God, but it does tell us enough so that we can relate to Him and live effectively. It is our true source of knowledge about the nature and heart of God. Our natural world may imply certain characteristics of God, but the Bible explains His heart. For example, most people looking at the awesome beauty and complexity of nature would admit that God is powerful and creative. Yet without the Bible, we would never know that God loves people so much that He was willing to leave the timelessness of heaven to live among us as a servant. We can see the power of creation in nature, but we would not see the power of the Cross without the Bible.

David wrote in Psalm 19:7-11:

> *The law of the Lord is perfect,*
> *reviving the soul.*
> *The statutes of the* LORD *are trustworthy,*
> *making wise the simple.*
> *The precepts of the* LORD *are right,*
> *giving joy to the heart.*
> *The commands of the* LORD *are radiant,*
> *giving light to the eyes.*
> *The fear of the* LORD *is pure,*
> *enduring forever.*
> *The ordinances of the* LORD *are sure*
> *and altogether righteous.*
> *They are more precious than gold,*
> *than much pure gold;*
> *they are sweeter than honey,*
> *than honey from the comb.*
> *By them is your servant warned;*
> *in keeping them there is great reward.* (NIV)

Q3. How did David describe God's Word?

Q4. What was David's conclusion about God's Word? How does that compare to your conclusion?

The Bible and Success

You can study the Bible like any other book in the library. You may have even tried to read parts of it in the past with mixed results. One unique characteristic of the Bible is that once you begin your faith journey with Christ, it becomes your word from God — a personal letter from your Father. Additionally, Jesus promised that the Holy Spirit would help us to understand it — and not just an academic or historical understanding, but a comprehension of the heart.

The apostle Paul wrote to new believers who had experienced the power of God's personal word, "And now we look back on all this and thank God, an artesian well of thanks! When you got the Message of God we preached, you didn't pass it off as just one more human opinion, but you took it to heart as God's true word to you, which it is, God himself at work in you believers!" (1 Thessalonians 2:13).

For followers of Christ, the Bible is more than an ancient book of stories — it's God's resource for sustaining their lives. I have heard people who recently began their faith walk say this about the Bible:

> "I tried reading the Bible before, but it was dry and boring. Now I read the same thing and it is alive and exciting."

> "I couldn't pick it up before, and now I can't put it down."

> "Before coming to Christ, the Bible was like reading someone else's mail. Now it's like having my own letter from God."

The Bible is God's primary means of speaking to us today. Reading and studying the Bible is how we develop a dialogue with God. God speaks to us through His Word, and we speak to Him through prayer. This two-way communication builds our relationship with Christ into something both personal and dynamic.

The Bible is like a how-to-live manual, a self-help book for life. It addresses not only spiritual issues but also earthly issues such as how to handle money or get along with a spouse. The Bible contains truth for conducting business as well as raising a family.

Paul summarized the importance and practical value of the Bible in his final letter to Timothy: "Every part of Scripture is God-breathed and useful one way or another — showing us truth, exposing our rebellion, correcting our mistakes, training us to live God's way. Through the Word we are put together and shaped up for the tasks God has for us" (2 Timothy 3:16-17).

> Q5. Based on this passage, what are four practical uses of the Bible, and how are they different?

There are many good translations of the Bible available today. We encourage you to get an inexpensive paperback version of the whole Bible and make it your own by reading it and marking in it. Highlighting words or phrases that stand out to you as you read is a good way to make the Bible personal.

The Bible and Obedience

The Bible was not given to increase our knowledge but to change our lives.
—D. L. Moody

Because the Bible was written in the context of real life, it contains facts of history, science, psychology, and geography. At a superficial level, this is valuable information. However, God's intent in giving us His Word was not only to bring us new information but also to give us truth to live by. It is in the understanding, belief, and application of Scripture that we discover its greatest value.

Jesus' most famous and comprehensive "how to live" message is recorded in Matthew 5–7. It is referred to as the Sermon on the Mount because Jesus presented it to a group of people gathered on a hillside. In this talk, Jesus described what it looks like to live as His follower. At the very end of His message, He told this famous story:

> "Therefore everyone who hears these words of mine and puts them into practice is like a wise man who built his house on the rock. The rain came down, the streams rose, and the winds blew and beat against that house; yet it did not fall,

because it had its foundation on the rock. But everyone who hears these words of mine and does not put them into practice is like a foolish man who built his house on sand. The rain came down, the streams rose, and the winds blew and beat against that house, and it fell with a great crash." (Matthew 7:24-27, NIV)

The Bible goes on to say that "when Jesus had finished saying these things, the crowds were amazed at his teaching, because he taught as one who had authority, and not as their teachers of the law" (7:28-29, NIV).

Q6. What do both of the homes in this story have in common?

Q7. What is different about the two builders?

Q8. What "big idea" was Jesus was trying to get across in this message?

There are five classical methods for getting a personal and practical grasp on the Bible. Each has a different dynamic and benefit, but they are equally important. These five methods are:

- Hearing: Listening to others as they share what they've learned from the Bible
- Reading: Reading the Bible to get an overview of its contents

- Studying: Focusing on small sections or ideas to gain in-depth understanding
- Memorizing: Committing short passages or verses to memory
- Meditating: Reflecting on the meaning of a verse, passage, or biblical idea over a period of time

As you continue your walk with Christ, learn to use each of these methods. Memorizing verses may sound difficult, but it can be a life-changing method for getting a grasp on the Bible. We suggest you begin by memorizing the key verses at the beginning of each lesson in this study.

Q9. What verse from this study will you memorize this week?

Suggestions for Memorizing Bible Verses

1. Identify a verse that is meaningful to you.

2. Write it on a 3 x 5 card. Include the reference.

3. Read it frequently.

4. Memorize it one phrase at a time until you can remember the whole statement.

5. Practice saying the verse from memory. Quote the reference at the beginning and end.

6. Review the verse every day for seven weeks.

7. Share the verse — and what it means to you — with a friend.

SUMMARY

The Bible is essential for our spiritual journey. It is more than a collection of stories or words of wisdom. It is God's letter to His people. It is absolutely true and reliable. It was supernaturally given and preserved. It will remain when man's wisdom has faded into history. Understanding, believing, and applying it to our lives is the only sure way to gain true meaning and success in this life.

PRAYER

Father, thank You that Your Word reveals who You are and guides my path. Teach me to trust in what You say and forgive me when I stray from it to go my own direction. Use Your Word to change my thinking, realign my values, and alter my behavior so that my life will honor You. Help me to live today in light of Your eternal truth.

LESSON 3

Prayer

NEXT STEPS

Prayer is the breath of the soul. It allows God access to our lives and needs. Prayer is an attitude of the heart that humbly admits the need for help and seeks the sunshine of God's grace. It is our personal communication with the living God.

> *"This is what I want you to do: Ask the Father for whatever is in keeping with the things I've revealed to you. Ask in my name, according to my will, and he'll most certainly give it to you. Your joy will be a river overflowing its banks!"*
>
> JOHN 16:23-24

George Mueller was the founder of the Ashley Down Orphanage in Bristol, England, during the late 1800s. With no resources except prayer and faith in God, Mr. Mueller saw God provide daily for the needs of his children.

One day as Mr. Mueller was traveling on a steamer to Quebec, the ship encountered a dense fog off the coast of Newfoundland. Mr. Mueller approached the captain and said, "Captain, I have come to tell you that I must be in Quebec on Saturday afternoon."

"That's impossible," the captain replied. "Do you know how dense this fog is?"

"No," Mueller replied, "my eye is not on the density of the fog but on the living God who controls every circumstance of my life."

Mr. Mueller prayed a simple prayer that would have been fitting in any child's Sunday school class. The burden of his prayer was something like this: "O Lord, if it is consistent with Your will, please remove this fog in five minutes. You know the engagement You made for me in Quebec for Saturday. I believe it is Your will."

The captain was also going to pray, but Mueller stopped him and said, "First, you do not believe God will do it; and second, I believe He has done it. And there is no need whatever for you to pray about it."

When they walked out of the chartroom, the fog was gone. By Saturday afternoon, Mr. Mueller was in Quebec.*

Prayer is a major resource for our walk with Christ. It is our moment-by-moment communication link with God. It is simple enough for a child to use yet so complex that great theologians don't fully understand it. It is practical yet a mystery.

Jesus expects us to pray. In this lesson we will look at some basic principles of prayer that will help you as you begin your walk with Christ.

Q1. Which of the following statements have been true of your thinking?
- _____ I pray only when I run out of my own resources and need help.
- _____ Prayer is for the religious part of my life.
- _____ Prayer requires a special vocabulary.
- _____ Prayer is a state of mind.
- _____ Prayer requires some merit on my part to be effective.
- _____ Prayer is like talking to myself.

In the Bible, prayer can refer to:

- Worship — Reflecting on who God is through praise
- Thanksgiving — Reviewing what God has done and expressing gratitude
- Confession — Admitting our failures and shortcomings
- Petition — Requesting help from God

Prayer is our part of a relational dialogue with God. Through the Scriptures, God speaks to us; through prayer, we speak to Him. Prayer can be formal or informal, private or public. It can be done in a church or in our homes. It can be done for hours or in a matter of seconds. It can be spoken or thought.

George Mueller: Man of Faith (Katong, Singapore: Warren Myers), p. 21; reprint of *An Hour with George Mueller*, ed. A. Sims (Grand Rapids, Mich.: Zondervan).

Prayer and Access

The writer of Hebrews said in Hebrews 4:14-16:

> Now that we know what we have — Jesus, this great High Priest with ready access to God — let's not let it slip through our fingers. We don't have a priest who is out of touch with our reality. He's been through weakness and testing, experienced it all — all but the sin. So let's walk right up to him and get what he is so ready to give. Take the mercy, accept the help.

The high priest was the top religious leader in the Old Testament form of worship. He was the only person who could go into the innermost part of the Old Testament tabernacle (the place of worship) — into the very presence of God. He was allowed to do this only once a year after elaborate preparations and sacrifices.

Q2. How is Jesus described in the previous passage?

Q3. Because of Christ's personal sacrifice, how is our relationship with God different from that of the people in Old Testament times?

In the Old Testament, few people spoke with God directly — most who did were prophets or priests. In part, this was because Old Testament rules stated that before a person could come into the presence of God, he must be spiritually clean. The elaborate system of Old Testament sacrifices was designed to connect a holy God with sinful men.

Jesus, as our High Priest, dealt with sin once and for all with His sacrifice on the cross. He gained access for us into the presence of God. Because of Jesus' action, we are encouraged to boldly enter into God's presence through prayer. Jesus earned this privilege for us, and it is one of the rights of being a child of God.

Prayer and Petitions

Prayer is a response to the knock of Christ at the door of our hearts (see Revelation 3:20). As we realize our need for Him and His desire to help, prayer becomes an invitation for His involvement. Prayer requires humility and faith. Humility says, "I have a need," and faith says, "I believe God can help."

Jesus gave the following teaching on prayer in Matthew 6:5-13. This passage is often called the Lord's Prayer, though it might more accurately be called "our" prayer because it shows us how we ought to pray.

> "And when you come before God, don't turn that into a theatrical production either. All these people making a regular show out of their prayers, hoping for stardom! Do you think God sits in a box seat?
>
> "Here's what I want you to do: Find a quiet, secluded place so you won't be tempted to role-play before God. Just be there as simply and honestly as you can manage. The focus will shift from you to God, and you will begin to sense his grace.
>
> "The world is full of so-called prayer warriors who are prayer-ignorant. They're full of formulas and programs and advice, peddling techniques for getting what you want from God. Don't fall for that nonsense. This is your Father you are dealing with, and he knows better than you what you need. With a God like this loving you, you can pray very simply. Like this:
>
>> Our Father in heaven,
>> Reveal who you are.
>> Set the world right;
>>   Do what's best —
>> as above, so below.
>> Keep us alive with three square meals.
>> Keep us forgiven with you and forgiving others.

> Keep us safe from ourselves and the Devil.
> You're in charge!
> You can do anything you want!
> You're ablaze in beauty!
>   Yes. Yes. Yes."

Imagine how surprised the disciples must have been when Jesus gave them a model for prayer that was so simple and short. It was likely in sharp contrast to the long-winded prayers they might have previously thought were proper. Yet in this brief prayer, we are taught the essentials of effective communication with God.

Q4. What does this passage tell us are the important components of prayer?

Q5. What instructions did Jesus give regarding prayer?

Did you notice that this prayer begins with a focus on God, moves to a focus on others, and ends with a focus on self? Effective prayer is not simply designed to meet our personal needs — giving God a "to do list." It encompasses so much more than that.

Prayer and God's Nature

Jesus told several parables (stories crafted to communicate specific lessons) to help people understand the value of prayer. One is found in Luke 11:5-13:

> Then he said, "Imagine what would happen if you went to a friend in the middle of the night and said, 'Friend, lend me

three loaves of bread. An old friend traveling through just showed up, and I don't have a thing on hand.'

"The friend answers from his bed, 'Don't bother me. The door's locked; my children are all down for the night; I can't get up to give you anything.'

"But let me tell you, even if he won't get up because he's a friend, if you stand your ground, knocking and waking all the neighbors, he'll finally get up and get you whatever you need.

"Here's what I'm saying:

Ask and you'll get;
Seek and you'll find;
Knock and the door will open."

God can be compared with the friend in the parable. Though God may at times appear to be reluctant to answer our prayers, He is actually causing us to ask, seek, and knock with our whole hearts. Could it be that our Father is inviting us to "bother" Him with our requests?

Q6. Knowing that God is eager to respond, is generous, and doesn't forget, why do you think He tells us to ask persistently or continually?

While we don't know the mystery behind prayer, there are many good reasons to pray. Praying strengthens our faith. As we continually come before God with our worship and needs, we learn to trust and rely on Him. We develop a new perspective and mindset. We move from independence to dependence.

As we persist in prayer, we also learn to listen to God. God is not like a heavenly Santa Claus giving us what we want at the moment we want it, but rather He works in our hearts to teach us to desire what is good and right. In prayer, God aligns the desires of our hearts to fit with His perfect plan. Consistent prayer also unleashes God's power. God has committed Himself to respond to the prayers of His people. Prayer is how we partner with God in doing what He wants done.

God answers prayer in one of three ways: "yes," "no," and "not yet." It's in the "not yet" that persistent prayer becomes most valuable. When we faithfully bring our needs to Him in prayer, He is not offended. In fact, He delights in our continued dependence.

Sometimes I pray as though God were a reluctant benefactor who needs to be convinced that what I'm asking for is worthwhile. In Luke 11:10-13, Jesus reminds us how we should think about God when we pray:

> "Don't bargain with God. Be direct. Ask for what you need. This is not a cat-and-mouse, hide-and-seek game we're in. If your little boy asks for a serving of fish, do you scare him with a live snake on his plate? If your little girl asks for an egg, do you trick her with a spider? As bad as you are, you wouldn't think of such a thing — you're at least decent to your own children. And don't you think the Father who conceived you in love will give the Holy Spirit when you ask him?"

Q7. What does this passage tell us about God's nature?

Q8. What keeps you from being bold and confident when praying?

Sometimes we become discouraged in prayer because we don't hear the answer we expect or want from God. But prayer is not a blank check written to pull from God's resources. And God is not a vending machine, dispensing His power at the push of a button. He is a wise God who knows *what* is best and *when* it is best.

God responds to our prayers for our ultimate benefit and for His glory. God uses prayer to accomplish two major goals: our joy and His will. The apostle John wrote in 1 John 5:14-15: "And how bold and free we then become in his presence, freely asking according to his will, sure that he's listening. And if we're confident that he's listening, we know that what we've asked for is as good as ours."

Q9. What does this passage teach us about prayer?

One of the best ways to keep prayer simple, consistent, and bold is to maintain a prayer list. A small, thin notebook or even a sheet of paper can serve as a handy system for jotting down prayers as well as a convenient way to record God's answers. Carry this notebook or paper with you so you can use it often.

SUMMARY

Prayer is more than a spiritual fire extinguisher. It is a privileged connection with the God of the universe. Prayer is a means to offer praise, give thanks, make requests, confess sins, and simply pour out our hearts to God. Our confidence in His willingness to hear and respond will give us the courage to keep our communication lines open with Him.

PRAYER

Thank You, Father, for the privilege of prayer. Thank You for being in touch with my every need. You know my deepest pain and my greatest joy. I know I can be honest with You because You know and accept me just as I am. Help me to bring each care and need to You for Your divine touch. Keep my habit of self-centeredness and independence from driving a wedge in our relationship. Help me to make prayer as natural to my spiritual journey as breathing is to my physical one.

LESSON 4

The Holy Spirit

NEXT STEPS

God's Spirit lives within each person who has received Christ by faith. Working with our spirits, the Holy Spirit teaches and comforts us as we journey through life with Christ. His presence brings us the ability to change our behavior and provides the power to live as we should.

> *"I will talk to the Father, and he'll provide you another Friend so that you will always have someone with you."*
> JOHN 14:16

On a family vacation in Colorado, we signed up for a whitewater rafting trip on the Arkansas River. We skipped over the first two difficulty levels and went straight for the "hang on to your lives" option.

We met our guide and then donned our iridescent wet suits, life preservers, and helmets. As we launched into the tranquil waters of the Arkansas River, our guide began a brief but important lecture and demonstration. His briefing included a litany of his qualifications: fifteen years' experience in rafting, leadership experience on every possible river in Colorado including the most difficult, six years' experience on this very river, and not a single passenger lost.

He then led our group in practicing the paddle maneuvers that would be critical once we reached the white water. We were instructed to respond to his commands instantly and vigorously. He explained that at times he would give different commands to each side of the raft that must be executed simultaneously. Finally, we were told what to do if someone fell overboard.

Then the whitewater adventure began in earnest. There were times when, looking ahead, I could see no way through the churning water and massive boulders that seemed to block our path. But each time, our guide strategically maneuvered us over, around, and through the obstacles. From his position at the stern of the raft, he calmly directed this novice crew safely through our scenic adventure.

God's Spirit is our expert guide through the "river" of life. He knows it well and promises to guide us safely over the rocks, around the boulders, and through the rough waters. He asks only that we listen, trust, and obey.

The Spirit and His Nature

God's Spirit, also called the Holy Spirit or the Spirit of Christ, is the third person of the Trinity. The first person is God the Father and the second is God the Son. Though the term *Trinity* is not used in the Bible, the concept is referenced throughout. It's okay if you don't fully understand how this works — it's a concept that is ultimately beyond human comprehension. It might help if you think of it as being similar to the way water works. Water, though a singular substance, can exist in three forms: liquid, solid (ice), and gas (steam). However, this is certainly an incomplete and inexact analogy.

In this lesson we will focus on the person of the Trinity called the Holy Spirit. While we can picture a father or a son, we don't have a complete picture of what a spirit looks like. This can lead people to see God's Spirit as simply a force rather than a person.

Yet the Bible relates all the personal attributes of God the Father and God the Son to the Spirit as well. The Spirit has a mind, emotions, and a will just like the Father and the Son. One of the definitions found in the dictionary for the word *person* is "a self-conscious or rational being."* The Bible does not describe the Holy Spirit as a mystical power or impersonal force. Rather He is a rational being — fully God and with a specific role in the lives of people.

Jesus taught His first followers about the Holy Spirit in John 16:12-15:

> "I still have many things to tell you, but you can't handle them now. But when the Friend comes, the Spirit of the Truth, he will take you by the hand and guide you into all the truth there is. He won't draw attention to himself, but will make sense out of what is about to happen and, indeed, out of all that I have done and said. He will honor me; he will take from me and deliver it to you. Everything the Father has is also mine. That is why I've said, 'He takes from me and delivers to you.'"

---

*The American College Dictionary, s.v. "Person."

L4

Q1. How is the Spirit of God described in this passage?

Q2. Read the passage again and note the various things the Holy Spirit does.

The Spirit of God is sometimes referred to as the Servant of the Trinity. In this role, He brings attention to God the Son and God the Father rather than bringing attention to Himself. His servant role does not in any way diminish the importance of His work or the need to understand His role in our lives, as we will see later in the study.

One of the promises that Christ made to those who put their faith in Him was that His Spirit would actually take up residence in their lives. Every believer is indwelt by God's Spirit, as explained in 1 Corinthians: "Don't you know that you yourselves are God's temple and that God's Spirit lives in you?" (3:16, NIV).

The Bible also says that we are baptized by the Spirit. The term *baptize* means "to place into." This term was used to describe the tempering of metal by placing it into water or the coloring of cloth by dipping it into a dye. Likewise, we are "placed into" the body of Christ by God's Spirit. In 1 Corinthians we read, "For we were all baptized by one Spirit into one body — whether Jews or Greeks, slave or free — and we were all given the one Spirit to drink" (12:13, NIV).

Learning to live in the reality of the indwelling Spirit of God is key to a successful life with Christ. His presence in us is more than a nice religious idea; it is absolutely critical to our relationship with God.

Q3. What practical difference does it make that God's Spirit lives in you?

Jesus promised that He would never leave His disciples. That would have been impossible throughout the centuries if His presence had remained limited to a physical body. Physically present, Jesus was limited by time and space. And so He left this world — in an event we call the Ascension — in order to send the Holy Spirit to dwell in all believers.

The Spirit and His Work

Our daughter was in her first musical production during her junior year of college. In preparation for her role, she read the script to understand the story and get to know her character. However, reading the script was just one aspect of the preparation needed for her performance. She also needed a director who could coach her on how to act, talk, and sing. The director was key to developing and blending the talents of each person into a performance that would honor the intent of the playwright and composer.

The Lord has given each of us a role to play in this life. It is a role filled with meaning and purpose. We learn our part as we study the Bible (the script). But we also need the Holy Spirit, who explains what we are to do and empowers us to do it. We can't honor the intent of our Creator without the power of the Spirit working in and through our lives.

As a new Christian, you may have some concerns regarding your ability to live the Christian life.

Q4. Put a mark next to any of the following statements that describe you:
   _____ I don't know if I'll ever understand the Bible.
   _____ Sometimes I don't know the right questions to ask.
   _____ My life is a tangled mess, and I can't change my old habits.
   _____ I try to live the right way, but I get tripped up and fail.

_____ I'm afraid that God's standards are too high and I won't be able to meet them.

_____ Other: _____

Our role, Jesus summarized, is to love God with all our hearts and to love our neighbors as ourselves. This is simple to say but impossible to do on our own. To accomplish this purpose, we need the constant coaching and empowering of God's Spirit. Jesus explained the role of God's Spirit in John 14:25-27:

> "I'm telling you these things while I'm still living with you. The Friend, the Holy Spirit whom the Father will send at my request, will make everything plain to you. He will remind you of all the things I have told you. I'm leaving you well and whole. That's my parting gift to you. Peace. I don't leave you the way you're used to being left — feeling abandoned, bereft. So don't be upset. Don't be distraught."

Q5. What did Jesus say the Spirit will do for you?

Q6. What do these verses say will be the result of God's Spirit at work within us?

Other people will come alongside you with a word of encouragement and direction as you live the life Jesus gave you. God designed the church (His followers) to be a resource on your journey. However, people aren't always there to help — and sometimes they simply let you down. God's Spirit is always present, always adequate, and always willing to guide and direct your life.

The Spirit and His Impact
God's Spirit not only leads and directs us; He also brings about real change.

Q7. As you read Romans 8:9-17, circle the things that change or are different when God's Spirit is in you.

> But if God himself has taken up residence in your life, you can hardly be thinking more of yourself than of him. Anyone, of course, who has not welcomed this invisible but clearly present God, the Spirit of Christ, won't know what we're talking about. But for you who welcome him, in whom he dwells — even though you still experience all the limitations of sin — you yourself experience life on God's terms. It stands to reason, doesn't it, that if the alive-and-present God who raised Jesus from the dead moves into your life, he'll do the same thing in you that he did in Jesus, bringing you alive to himself? When God lives and breathes in you (and he does, as surely as he did in Jesus), you are delivered from that dead life. With his Spirit living in you, your body will be as alive as Christ's!
>
> So don't you see that we don't owe this old do-it-yourself life one red cent. There's nothing in it for us, nothing at all. The best thing to do is give it a decent burial and get on with your new life. God's Spirit beckons. There are things to do and places to go!
>
> This resurrection life you received from God is not a timid, grave-tending life. It's adventurously expectant, greeting God with a childlike "What's next, Papa?" God's Spirit touches our spirits and confirms who we really are. We know who he is, and we know who we are: Father and children. And we know we are going to get what's coming to us — an unbelievable inheritance! We go through exactly what Christ goes through. If we go through the hard times with him, then we're certainly going to go through the good times with him!

Wherever the Spirit of God is, there is power. Jesus explained it to His early disciples like this: "But you will receive power when the Holy Spirit has come upon you; and you shall be My witnesses both in Jerusalem, and in all

Judea and Samaria, and even to the remotest part of the earth" (Acts 1:8, NASB).

God's Spirit brings power to live life as God designed it. His Spirit brings inside-out change. He actually changes us to reflect His character and nature. Over time we will bear the family likeness more and more, as described in 2 Corinthians 3:18: "And we, who with unveiled faces all reflect the Lord's glory, are being transformed into his likeness with ever-increasing glory, which comes from the Lord, who is the Spirit" (NIV).

The apostle Paul described this change to reflect God's likeness as bearing the "fruit of the Spirit." Paul gave a list of these character qualities in Galatians 5:22-23: "But the fruit of the Spirit is love, joy, peace, patience, kindness, goodness, faithfulness, gentleness and self-control. Against such things there is no law" (NIV).

The term *fruit* provides a word picture of the character change in a Christian as a result of the work of the Spirit. To understand this word picture, we can reflect on the nature of fruit as we know it in the natural world. Consider these "fruit facts":

1. Each tree naturally bears only one type of fruit.
2. The amount of fruit a tree is able to produce depends on:
   a. The maturity of the tree
   b. The amount of nutrients available and absorbed
   c. The presence or absence of disease
3. A deep root system gives a fruit tree greater access to water and stability.

These facts of nature give us insight into how we can cooperate with God's Spirit so that His fruit (a spiritual nature) is produced in our lives.

Christians should expect to produce the fruit of the Spirit because they have the reality of the Spirit within them. Loving our enemies, the unlovable, or the ungrateful, for example, is an unselfish kind of love that comes only from the nature of God. In order to produce spiritual fruit, we need to:

1. Grow in maturity
2. Take in the nourishment of God's Word
3. Deal with the presence of sin that robs us of spiritual health

Spiritual fruit will grow when we develop deep spiritual roots in Christ and His Word. These roots will provide strength and stability in difficult times.

For the Spirit of God to change us, we not only need to acknowledge His presence in our lives, but we also need to actively cooperate with Him by following His directions and relying on His supernatural power. We will do well to follow the advice given in Proverbs 3:5-6:

> *Trust GOD from the bottom of your heart;*
> *don't try to figure out everything on your own.*
> *Listen for GOD's voice in everything you do, everywhere you go;*
> *he's the one who will keep you on track.*

Q8. What are specific ways you can cooperate with the Spirit of God?

Q9. How has God changed your life since you put your faith in Him?

Q10. What are some things you would like to see change in the future as you continue your journey with Christ?

SUMMARY

God lives in us through His Spirit. His presence means that we are never alone. God's Spirit is always available to guide, direct, and comfort us along the journey. As we respond to His presence, we are changed into His likeness. That likeness will increasingly reflect the true nature and character of God.

PRAYER

Father, thank You for the way Your Spirit works in my life. Thank You that He gives me an understanding of who You are and helps me to live a life that honors You. On my own I would fail, but You have filled me with Your presence so I am never alone. Help me to listen to Your Spirit and treat people today with love and kindness.

LESSON 5

Grace

NEXT STEPS

Grace is an amazing truth that God accepts us, not because of what we have done, but because of what Christ did for us. Grace is the foundation for our security with God, the source of forgiveness, and the power to live as we should. Grace is the atmosphere that enables us to experience freedom in our relationship with Jesus.

> *God . . . has saved us and called us to a holy life—not because of anything we have done but because of his own purpose and grace. This grace was given us in Christ Jesus before the beginning of time.*
> 2 TIMOTHY 1:8-9, NIV

King David is one of the most famous Old Testament characters in the Bible. The second king of Israel, he was called a man after God's own heart (see Acts 13:22). As a young man he delivered Israel from oppression when he killed a giant warrior with his slingshot (remember Goliath?). He was anointed by God to be king of Israel and then spent the next ten years as a fugitive, running from the current king, King Saul. David finally became king at the age of thirty after years of self-exile in caves and the desert.

After King David set up his administration, he did an amazing, countercultural act. He asked his advisors, "Is there no one still left of the house of Saul to whom I can show God's kindness?" (2 Samuel 9:3, NIV). Rather than eliminate any possible competition from the previous king—a king who had threatened to kill him—David wanted to honor Saul's descendants. He found just one relative: a grandson of King Saul named Mephibosheth, who had become permanently injured while escaping the aftermath of King Saul's demise. For years he had been hiding, fearing reprisal from a new king and his party.

King David demonstrated grace rather than retribution in dealing with this grandson of King Saul. He restored Mephibosheth's family wealth, provided managers for his land, and invited him into the royal family circle as a permanent honored guest (see 2 Samuel 9).

King David reflected the grace of God in his attitude and actions to this surprised young man. All Mephibosheth had to do was accept it!

Grace and Acceptance

In most settings, the basis of acceptance is performance. Business, education, and sports all operate based on performance. You either do your job well or you're let go; you win or you don't play. Value is primarily determined by how well you do what you are called to do. Merit, in its various forms, is the fuel that drives the engine of success and acceptance.

The Bible introduces a radically different definition of value: the concept of grace, or unmerited favor. The phrase *kindness of God* is used in the Old Testament to communicate God's grace. Showing grace means to give favor to someone who doesn't deserve it and would never be able to earn it.

> **Q1.** Describe a situation or environment you've been in that was based on grace instead of merit. How did it make you feel?

We thrive on merit. We love the challenge to outperform others. We like to assert our abilities and experience pride in what we do. Why? Because we can take credit for the results. Merit keeps us in the driver's seat. We are in control. Merit and performance are key to world religions too — every religion *except* Christianity.

But even in Christianity, people often get it wrong — they try to get to heaven based on their good behavior. When asked, "Why should God let you into heaven?" many people respond, "Because the good that I have done is greater than the bad!" In other words, they believe they have earned it. As Pastor Bill Hybels puts it, the message of Christ is "done," not "do." Christ did it all, and there is nothing left for us to do.

In order to better understand grace, it's important to understand God's holiness and love. God's holiness means that He can't tolerate sin. His love means that He is deeply compassionate and forgiving. God's holiness and love are like the two parts of a cross: His holiness is the vertical piece and His love the horizontal. Where the two meet is grace, the divine connection between absolute holiness and unconditional love.

Suppose a UPS driver comes up to your door and hands you a package worth more than you could ever earn in a lifetime. He tells you that it is addressed to you from an anonymous benefactor and that there are no strings attached. All you have to do is sign the form saying you received it. You could refuse the package, unwilling to accept it unless you could do something to earn it. Or you could sign your name on the form, fully believing you did earn it. Both actions would be unexpected and unlikely. Perhaps instead, even though you knew you didn't deserve it, you would accept the gift.

God's gift of life is worth more than you could ever earn in many lifetimes. He offers it to you with no strings attached and simply waits for you to accept it. Paul summed it up like this in Ephesians 2:8-9: "Saving is all his idea, and all his work. All we do is trust him enough to let him do it. It's God's gift [grace] from start to finish! We don't play the major role. If we did, we'd probably go around bragging that we'd done the whole thing!"

Q2. When it comes to grace, what is God's role and what is our role?

It's not unusual for people who begin their walk with Christ by accepting God's unmerited favor to soon feel they must perform in order to keep His favor.

Q3. What does the previous passage from Ephesians say about continuing your walk with Christ by grace?

It's easy for merit-thinking to creep into our relationship with Christ. When we are performing well (praying often, reading the Bible regularly, serving others selflessly), we may feel as if we have a greater audience with God. Yet God's grace means that we are at *no time* more acceptable to Him than when we first came to faith. We can't earn a better standing in the environment of grace.

In God's family, grace is a relational environment in which we are initially and permanently accepted. Grace, however, doesn't eliminate work, service, and obedience. In God's environment of grace we don't work or obey *to earn* God's favor, but we obey *because of* God's favor. The difference is significant. In the former, we are driven by performance, self-promotion, or fear. In the latter, we are motivated by thankfulness and gratitude.

Grace and Forgiveness

On our journey with Christ we will still face detours, wrong turns, and dead ends. What happens when we lose our way, take the wrong road, or wind up in a moral cul-de-sac?

Q4. Describe a time when you got lost. How did you feel? What did you do?

In our walk with Christ, sin causes us to get lost. Sin is failing to do what God desires or doing something that separates us from God. It means missing the mark of God's target. Sin is a big deal to God even if it is not regarded as such in our culture. When we come to faith in Christ, God forgives our sin — past, present, and future. Sin is no longer held against us; our record is wiped clean by the blood of Christ. But although sin no longer affects our *acceptance* with God, it does affect our *relationship* with Him. Read what the apostle John wrote about sin in 1 John 1:5-10:

This, in essence, is the message we heard from Christ and are passing on to you: God is light, pure light; there's not a trace of darkness in him.

If we claim that we experience a shared life with him and continue to stumble around in the dark, we're obviously lying through our teeth — we're not *living* what we claim. But if we walk in the light, God himself being the light, we also experience a shared life with one another, as the sacrificed blood of Jesus, God's Son, purges all our sin.

If we claim that we're free of sin, we're only fooling ourselves. A claim like that is errant nonsense. On the other hand, if we admit our sins — make a clean breast of them — he won't let us down; he'll be true to himself. He'll forgive our sins and purge us of all wrongdoing. If we claim that we've never sinned, we out-and-out contradict God — make a liar out of him. A claim like that only shows off our ignorance of God.

Q5. What does this passage say we should do about our sin?

Q6. What does God say He will do?

Q7. Read the following passage from 1 John. According to these verses, what are the primary sources of sin?

> Don't love the world's ways. Don't love the world's goods. Love of the world squeezes out love for the Father. Practically everything that goes on in the world — wanting your own

way, wanting everything for yourself, wanting to appear important — has nothing to do with the Father. It just isolates you from him. (2:15-16)

Luke recorded an interesting event in the life of Christ in Luke 7:36-50:

> One of the Pharisees asked him over for a meal. He went to the Pharisee's house and sat down at the dinner table. Just then a woman of the village, the town harlot, having learned that Jesus was a guest in the home of the Pharisee, came with a bottle of very expensive perfume and stood at his feet, weeping, raining tears on his feet. Letting down her hair, she dried his feet, kissed them, and anointed them with the perfume. When the Pharisee who had invited him saw this, he said to himself, "If this man was the prophet I thought he was, he would have known what kind of woman this is who is falling all over him."
>
> Jesus said to him, "Simon, I have something to tell you."
>
> "Oh? Tell me."
>
> "Two men were in debt to a banker. One owed five hundred silver pieces, the other fifty. Neither of them could pay up, and so the banker canceled both debts. Which of the two would be more grateful?"
>
> Simon answered, "I suppose the one who was forgiven the most."
>
> "That's right," said Jesus. Then turning to the woman, but speaking to Simon, he said, "Do you see this woman? I came to your home; you provided no water for my feet, but she rained tears on my feet and dried them with her hair. You gave me no greeting, but from the time I arrived she hasn't quit kissing my feet. You provided nothing for freshening up, but she has soothed my feet with perfume. Impressive, isn't

it? She was forgiven many, many sins, and so she is very, very grateful. If the forgiveness is minimal, the gratitude is minimal."

Then he spoke to her: "I forgive your sins."

That set the dinner guests talking behind his back: "Who does he think he is, forgiving sins!"

He ignored them and said to the woman, "Your faith has saved you. Go in peace."

Q8. What do you learn about forgiveness from this passage?

Q9. How does this story demonstrate grace?

GRACE AND POWER

The term *grace* in the Bible also implies power. It is God's grace that frees us from being ruled by sin and begins to change us from the inside out. It is the grace of God that enables us to live as we should. Paul said in Philippians 2:12-13: "Therefore, my dear friends, as you have always obeyed — not only in my presence, but now much more in my absence — continue to work out your salvation with fear and trembling, for it is God who works in you to will and to act according to his good purpose" (NIV).

God not only empowers us to do what He wants but also gives us the desire to do it. God's grace in our lives changes our values and motives. The journey with Christ is not a matter of self-effort focused in a spiritual direction but of God's effort leading, guiding, and energizing every aspect of our lives.

L5

Paul made an exciting discovery along his journey with Christ, but that discovery first appeared to him to be an inconvenient and unnecessary burden. Read what he discovered in 2 Corinthians 12:7-10:

> Because of the extravagance of those revelations, and so I wouldn't get a big head, I was given the gift of a handicap to keep me in constant touch with my limitations. Satan's angel* did his best to get me down; what he in fact did was push me to my knees. No danger then of walking around high and mighty! At first I didn't think of it as a gift, and begged God to remove it. Three times I did that, and then he told me,
> *My grace is enough; it's all you need.*
> *My strength comes into its own in your weakness.*
> Once I heard that, I was glad to let it happen. I quit focusing on the handicap and began appreciating the gift. It was a case of Christ's strength moving in on my weakness. Now I take limitations in stride, and with good cheer, these limitations that cut me down to size — abuse, accidents, opposition, bad breaks. I just let Christ take over! And so the weaker I get, the stronger I become.

Q10. What did Paul discover about God's grace?

Q11. What change in perspective occurred when Paul understood the significance of grace?

---

*Satan has many spirits that follow him. These are sometimes called demons or fallen angels.

Q12. Describe a time in your life when you felt like Paul did upon receiving his "gift of a handicap." How could (or did) grace help you deal with your situation?

SUMMARY

Grace is real, but we can't earn what God freely gives. We can only accept it. Our walk with God is powered by His unmerited favor. It surrounds, supports, and enables us to walk with Him in freedom. Instead of basing our relationship with God on our work or performance, we can accept the gift of salvation given to us through Christ's death on the cross and enjoy His environment of grace.

PRAYER

Thank You, Father, for accepting me in Christ. Thank You that my journey with You starts and ends with Your grace. Supported by Your unmerited favor, I never need to fear rejection. I am always secure with You. Help me to live today with an attitude of thankfulness for what You have done.

LESSON 6

Community

NEXT STEPS

God has designed His followers to live and travel with companions in community. Christ leads this community (the church) and bonds it together through love. Each person has a significant and unique part to play within the whole community. Learning from and supporting each other is crucial for a successful journey.

> *Two can accomplish more than twice as much as one, for the results can be much better. If one falls, the other pulls him up; but if a man falls when he is alone, he's in trouble. Also, on a cold night, two under the same blanket gain warmth from each other, but how can one be warm alone? And one standing alone can be attacked and defeated, but two can stand back-to-back and conquer; three is even better, for a triple-braided cord is not easily broken.*
> ECCLESIASTES 4:9-12, TLB

Aron Ralston is an avid outdoorsman in excellent physical condition and a veteran climber of over one hundred of Colorado's highest peaks. In April 2003, Aron went on a one-day climb in a remote area of southeastern Utah . . . alone.

Forty miles from the nearest paved road and sixty feet up on a sheer rock face, Aron's right arm became pinned beneath a thousand-pound shifting boulder. Five days after becoming trapped and forty hours after he'd run out of water, he made a critical decision. His only hope for survival was to cut off his own arm. Using a pocketknife, he amputated his arm just below the elbow, applied a tourniquet, and then rappelled sixty feet to the canyon floor. After walking for several hours, he met other hikers who helped bring in lifesaving medical assistance.

Our journey with Christ is too difficult and too dangerous to go solo. God never intended us to travel alone but rather with companions — in community — with each member supporting and contributing to the journey.

Community and Companionship

As Jesus prepared His followers for the future, He taught them to seek one quality — a quality that would become the hallmark of His touch on their lives. He said in John 13:34-35, "Let me give you a new command: Love one another. In the same way I loved you, you love one another. This is how everyone will recognize that you are my disciples — when they see the love you have for each other."

Some years later, Paul commended new believers in Thessalonica for this very quality: "You need to know, friends, that thanking God over and over for you is not only a pleasure; it's a must. We *have* to do it. Your faith is growing phenomenally; your love for each other is developing wonderfully. Why, it's only right that we give thanks" (2 Thessalonians 1:3).

Paul also gave a description of the kind of love that Jesus was talking about in 1 Corinthians 13:1-7.

Q1. As you read this classic description of love, circle what love does and underline what love does not do.

> If I speak with human eloquence and angelic ecstasy but don't love, I'm nothing but the creaking of a rusty gate.
> If I speak God's Word with power, revealing all his mysteries and making everything plain as day, and if I have faith that says to a mountain, "Jump," and it jumps, but I don't love, I'm nothing.
> If I give everything I own to the poor and even go to the stake to be burned as a martyr, but I don't love, I've gotten nowhere. So, no matter what I say, what I believe, and what I do, I'm bankrupt without love.
>   Love never gives up.
>   Love cares more for others than for self.
>   Love doesn't want what it doesn't have.
>   Love doesn't strut,
>   Doesn't have a swelled head,
>   Doesn't force itself on others,

Isn't always "me first,"
Doesn't fly off the handle,
Doesn't keep score of the sins of others,
Doesn't revel when others grovel,
Takes pleasure in the flowering of truth,
Puts up with anything,
Trusts God always,
Always looks for the best,
Never looks back,
But keeps going to the end. (1 Corinthians 13:1-7)

Q2. How does this description of love compare with the way our culture defines love?

The Bible uses different words for love. One (*phileo*) refers to friendship — love that results because we admire someone or enjoy the company of that person. Another (*agape*) refers to a sacrificial love — love that is offered unconditionally. This has also been called divine love because it is the kind of love God has for us.

God wants this kind of agape love to permeate all of our relationships. In the community of believers, it is a love that builds immediate closeness. You will be amazed at the kindred spirit you enjoy with other followers of Christ, even though you may not know them well. Outside the community of believers, it is a love that helps to identify you as God's child.

COMMUNITY AND CONTRIBUTION

The book of Acts records the beginning of the church and, more specifically, how Christ-followers began to experience community. In Acts 2, Peter presented the message of Christ to a large group of people. Thousands of them put their faith in Christ and became His followers. In doing so, they discovered a new and powerful support system. People who didn't know each other found a common bond and encouragement as they enjoyed community together.

Q3. Read the following account from Acts 2:41-47 and describe the spiritual and physical support these new believers found in community.

> That day about three thousand took him at his word, were baptized and were signed up. They committed themselves to the teaching of the apostles, the life together, the common meal, and the prayers.
> Everyone around was in awe — all those wonders and signs done through the apostles! And all the believers lived in a wonderful harmony, holding everything in common. They sold whatever they owned and pooled their resources so that each person's need was met.
> They followed a daily discipline of worship in the Temple followed by meals at home, every meal a celebration, exuberant and joyful, as they praised God. People in general liked what they saw. Every day their number grew as God added those who were saved.

Q4. What were the results of this new community?

These early believers discovered that they could accomplish more together than they could alone. They also discovered that they needed each other. Throughout his letters, Paul reminded new believers that this community, the church (also called the "body of Christ" or the "body of believers"), is a unique and essential part of the faith journey.

Football provides us with a good analogy of how we work together in

Christ's body. We are one team yet many players. Some positions may be more visible than others, yet all are equally important. A good coach assigns positions according to each player's physical design. Each player has a specific role that when carried out makes the team successful.

In a similar manner, every believer is essential to the team we call the church. As you walk with Christ, you will discover that you have special spiritual abilities. The Holy Spirit gave these gifts to you when you became a believer, and they will allow you to make a unique contribution to the community of believers.

COMMUNITY AND INFLUENCE

As we walk with Christ, there is a great deal to learn. We can learn much from fellow travelers — especially those who have been traveling a little longer than we have. Paul knew the importance of this kind of personal influence and how it helped with the development and training of new believers. Timothy was a young apprentice who often traveled with Paul. At the close of his life, Paul wrote a letter to Timothy in which he praised Timothy for learning from the influence of others during his spiritual journey. Here's an excerpt from that letter:

> But you know from watching me that I am not that kind of person. You know what I believe and the way I live and what I want. You know my faith in Christ and how I have suffered. You know my love for you, and my patience. You know how many troubles I have had as a result of my preaching the Good News. You know about all that was done to me while I was visiting in Antioch, Iconium, and Lystra, but the Lord delivered me. Yes, and those who decide to please Christ Jesus by living godly lives will suffer at the hands of those who hate him. In fact, evil men and false teachers will become worse and worse, deceiving many, they themselves having been deceived by Satan.
>
> But you must keep on believing the things you have been taught. You know they are true, for you know that you can trust those of us who have taught you. You know how, when you were a small child, you were taught the holy Scriptures; and it is these that make you wise to accept God's salvation by trusting in Christ Jesus. (2 Timothy 3:10-15, TLB)

Q5. What were some of the things Timothy learned from Paul?

Timothy also had others who influenced his life. Two are mentioned in 2 Timothy 1:5: "That precious memory triggers another: your honest faith — and what a rich faith it is, handed down from your grandmother Lois to your mother Eunice, and now to you!"

Q6. Who have been significant influences in your Christian walk?

Q7. Who do you know who could be a "Paul," or a mentor, to you as you continue your spiritual journey?

Ask God to bring into your life someone whom you respect for his or her spiritual faith. Then be courageous and ask this person to consider being a mentor for you in your spiritual journey. The role of a mentor isn't simply to teach you; it is to teach you so that you can then teach others. Read what Paul revealed about the purpose of mentoring in 2 Timothy 2:2: "And the things you have heard me say in the presence of many witnesses entrust to reliable men who will also be qualified to teach others" (NIV).

Timothy was not only personally mentored by Paul, but his apprenticeship occurred in the context of community. In that community, Timothy had three types of relationships: with a mentor, with his peers, and with those he taught. Paul told Timothy not only to be a learner but also to become a teacher. Timothy was to be a spiritual link in a chain of learners and fellow travelers.

As you continue to grow in your relationship with Christ and in your understanding and application of the Bible, look for someone you can influence — perhaps a friend who is interested in how you got started on your journey with Christ. At some point in your journey, you will meet someone who is what you are now: a new believer. Your walk with Christ can offer wisdom and encouragement to that believer. Hang on to this book. You may even want to use it (and the others in this series) to help guide this new believer.

May God be with you as you continue your walk of faith.

SUMMARY

God designed us to travel our spiritual journey in the companionship of others. This community of believers is uniquely bonded together by the power of love. Living in community, we are interdependent — we need each other to finish the journey successfully.

PRAYER

Thank You, Father, that I don't have to travel this journey alone. You have given me traveling companions to share with and learn from. Teach me to love my companions as You love me. Help me to be a spiritual link in the chain of relationships that will build up Your community of faith.

Summary

*U*se the following chart to review the lessons you have just completed. You may want to show someone else what you have been learning about your journey with Christ.

LESSON	KEY VERSE	SCRIPTURES	KEY CONCEPTS
Faith 1	Proverbs 3:5-6	Hebrews 11:1 Hebrews 11:6 Luke 8:40-56	• **Faith and Reality** • Faith and God • Faith and Action
The Word 2	Psalm 119:19-20	Psalm 19:7-11 2 Timothy 3:16-17 Matthew 7:24-27	• **The Bible and Truth** • The Bible and Success • The Bible and Obedience
Prayer 3	John 16:23-24	Hebrews 4:14-16 Matthew 6:5-13 Luke 11:5-13	• **Prayer and Access** • Prayer and Petitions • Prayer and God's Nature
The Holy Spirit 4	John 14:16	John 16:12-15 John 14:25-27 Romans 8:9-17	• **The Spirit and His Nature** • The Spirit and His Work • The Spirit and His Impact
Grace 5	2 Timothy 1:8-9	Ephesians 2:8-9 Luke 7:36-50 2 Corinthians 12:7-10	• **Grace and Acceptance** • Grace and Forgiveness • Grace and Power
Community 6	Ecclesiastes 4:9-12	1 Corinthians 13:1-7 Acts 2:41-47 2 Timothy 3:10-15	• **Community and Companionship** • Community and Contribution • Community and Influence

About the Authors

Ron and Mary Bennett joined the staff of The Navigators in 1970. They have led ministries on college campuses, in the military, and in the community. They are currently part of the national leadership team of the Church Discipleship Ministry (CDM) within The Navigators. Ron serves as director of the Strategic Resource Group for CDM. He is the author of *Intentional Disciplemaking* and a coauthor of *Opening the Door* and *The Adventure of Discipling Others*.

The *Beginning the Walk* studies were developed by The Navigators' Church Discipleship Ministry (CDM). CDM serves local churches by helping them develop into intentional disciplemaking communities. This series is part of a group of resources that can help equip your church to make disciples. For more information on The Navigators' Church Discipleship Ministry resources, go to www.navigators.org/cdm.

www.ingramcontent.com/pod-product-compliance
Lightning Source LLC
Chambersburg PA
CBHW071222070526
44584CB00019B/3126